ShortCuts

FOR WINTER

Teacher Timesaver Charts, Patterns, Awards,
Newsletter, Calendars, Name Tags, Worksheets, and More

by Marilynn G. Barr

Monday Morning is a registered trademark of
Monday Morning Books, Inc.

Entire contents copyright © 1992
by Monday Morning Books, Inc., Box 1680,
Palo Alto, California 94302

For a complete catalog write to the address above.

ISBN 1-878279-44-0

Printed in the United States of America

Contents

4   Introduction

Open House Door Displays
5   December
6   January
7   February

Bulletin Board Displays
8   December
10   January
12   February

Bulletin Board Characters
14   Mouse
15   Penguin
16   Polar Bear
17   Seal
18   Snowman
19   Teddy Bear

Bulletin Board Borders
20   December
21   January
22   February

Notes
23   Take-Home Progress Notes
24   Thank You Notes
25   Homework Reminders
26   Open Notes to Parent
27   Open Letter to Parents

Planning Calendars
28   December
29   January
30   February

Weekly Calendar Friezes
31   December
32   January
33   February

Birthday Charts
34   December
36   January
38   February

Scrapbook Pages
40   December
41   January
42   February

Seating Charts
43   December
44   January
45   February

Attendance Charts
46   December
47   January
48   February
49   Open Chart
50   Substitute Teacher Agenda

Open Manuscript Worksheets
51   December
52   January
53   February

Open Shape Worksheets
54   December
55   January
56   February

Worksheet Display Banners
57   December
58   January
59   February

Newsletter Artwork
60   Cover
61   Section Titles

File Folder Covers
62   December
63   January
64   February

Name Tags/Flashcards
65   December
66   January
67   February
68   Doorknob Hanger & Hall Passes

Bookmarks
69   Good Books to Read!
70   My Favorite Books!
71   I Love Books!

Awards
72   Pencil Awards
73   Button Awards
75   Headband/Wristband Awards
76   Club Card & Coupon Awards
77   Booklet Award

Diplomas
78   Big Snowflake Diploma
79   Winter Wonderland Diploma
80   Big Valentine Diploma

Introduction

Rewarding your students' achievements, scheduling parent-teacher conferences, and preparing for open house are easy with the seasonal patterns, charts, open worksheets, worksheet display banners, substitute teacher agenda, name tags, file folder covers, awards, and diplomas in **ShortCuts for Winter**.

Celebrate the New Year with the January Open House Door Display, Bulletin Board Displays, and Bulletin Board Characters and Borders on pages 6, 10-11, 14-19, and 21. Accompanying Birthday, Seating, and Attendance Charts make it easy to get excited about the new year!

Bulletin Board Characters are designed to use with the name tags/flashcards for a hands-on skills practice bulletin board or to display spelling words, math facts, color words, numerals, etc. Duplicate enough characters for each student in your class. Have each child color and cut out his or her character and attach a straw or paint stirrer to the back for a hand puppet.

The Bulletin Board Borders are easy to cut out and can be used to frame bulletin board displays. They can also be made into student headbands for class plays, parties, or just for fun. To make headbands, supply each child with three strips of the same border. Have students color and cut out the strips and tape or staple together the ends to form a band to fit each child's head. For a new twist, have your class color enough strips to decorate the window frames in your classroom to match the bulletin board border.

The variety of notes on pages 23-27 can be used to correspond with parents.

Provide your students with Weekly Calendar Friezes (pages 31-33) to take home for parents to keep track of happenings in school. Or, provide calendars for each child to keep track of weekly weather changes.

List children's birth dates on the two-piece Birthday Charts on pages 34-38. As an alternative, eliminate the messages and use these charts to list classroom helpers, super achievers, and citizenship recognition or to announce a special event or guest.

Scrapbook Pages are a favorite with children and parents. Have your students periodically color or cut out pictures of favorite things, memorable events, parties, and special interests to paste on the Scrapbook Pages. Or have each student use the pages to make a keepsake record of skills practice, achievements, and awards to bind between construction paper covers and decorate.

Double the use of each Seating Chart as a trail gameboard. Before reproducing, write Start at one corner, End at the opposite corner, and program a few spaces with rewards and/or consequences. Color the repeating pattern and supply pawns and a spinner or skills practice game cards. Children then play the game similar to the way they play Candyland.

You can also double the use of the Attendance Charts by creating crossword puzzles or maze games for your students. Eliminate each heading and paste a Bulletin Board Border strip over the listing column to dress up the crossword or maze.

Program the Open Worksheets on pages 51-56 for skills practice. Eliminate the lines on the Open Manuscript Worksheets and use as bulletin board displays, picture frames, or art project frames. For a rainy day filler activity, provide each child with his or her own Open Shape Worksheet, paste, and colored tissue paper. Have students tear the tissue paper into small pieces and paste them inside the shape. Overlapping the tissue creates a stained-glass effect and makes an attractive display for windows, bulletin boards, and seasonal take-home gifts.

Worksheet Display Banners make "good work" displays extra special. You can also eliminate the messages and use the banners to display seasonal posters, student of the week photographs, or classroom rules.

Newsletters that let parents know all about what their child's class is doing are easy to produce with the Newsletter Covers and Section Titles on pages 60-61. The artwork is also a great companion to the Scrapbook Pages for a classroom annual filled with memories.

In addition to identifying types of work, File Folder Covers can also be used as mini seasonal coloring posters. To do this, eliminate the words and provide students with crayons and/or markers to color and decorate their posters.

Open House Door Display

December

Happy Holidays!
from

_____'s
Teacher

Class

Open House Door Display

We Wish You A Joyous New Year!

_____ 'Class

Teacher

HAPPY VALENTINE'S DAY

from _____ 's Class.

Teacher

Bulletin Board Displays
December

Bulletin Board Displays
December

Bulletin Board Displays

January

Bulletin Board Displays

January

Bulletin Board Displays
February

ShortCuts for Winter ©1992 Monday Morning Books, Inc.

Bulletin Board Displays

February

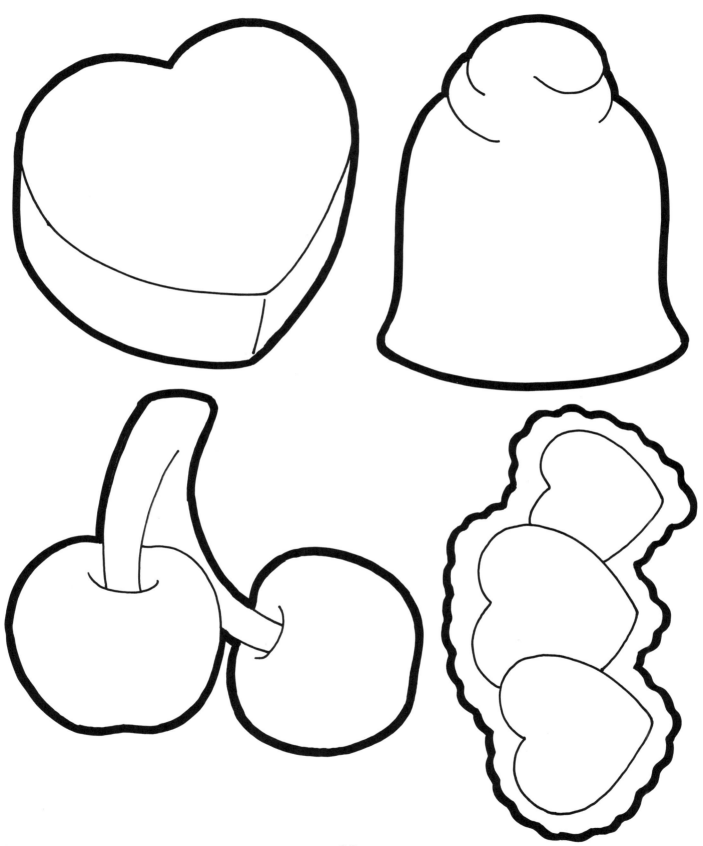

Bulletin Board Character
Mouse

Bulletin Board Character

Penguin

Bulletin Board Character
Polar Bear

Bulletin Board Character
Seal

ShortCuts for Winter ©1992 Monday Morning Books, Inc.

Bulletin Board Character
Snowman

Bulletin Board Character
Teddy Bear

Bulletin Board Borders
December

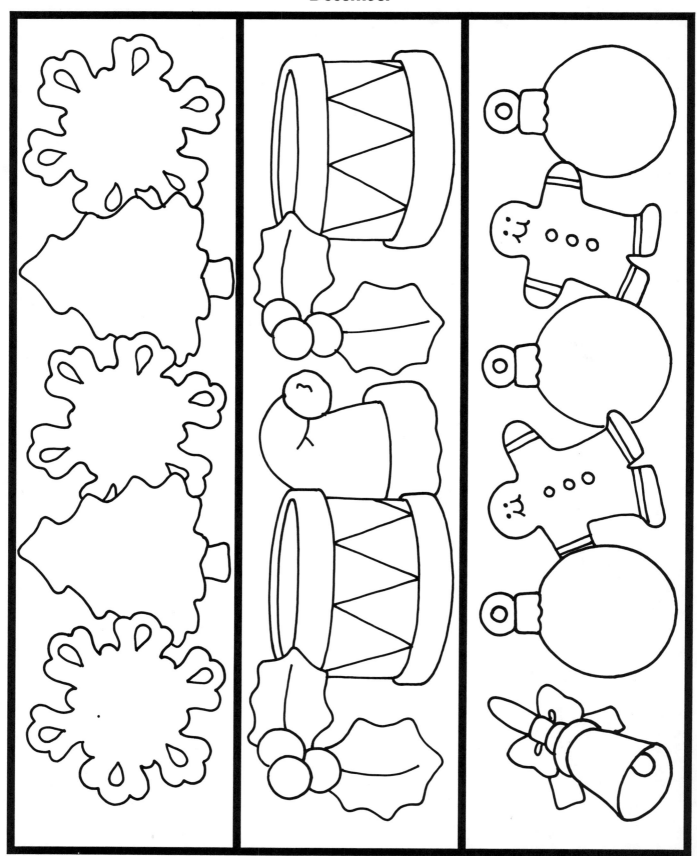

Bulletin Board Borders
January

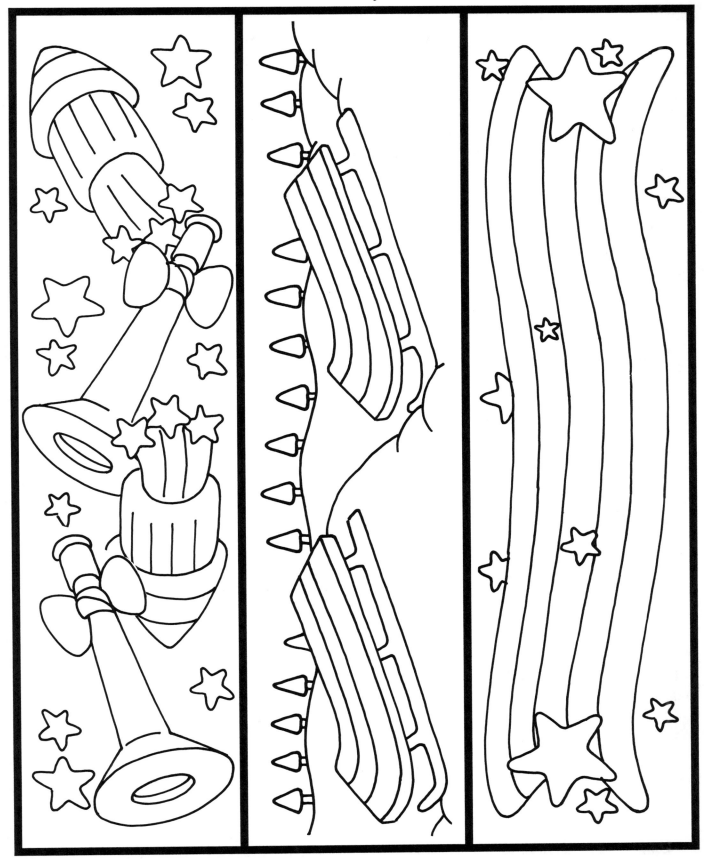

Bulletin Board Borders

February

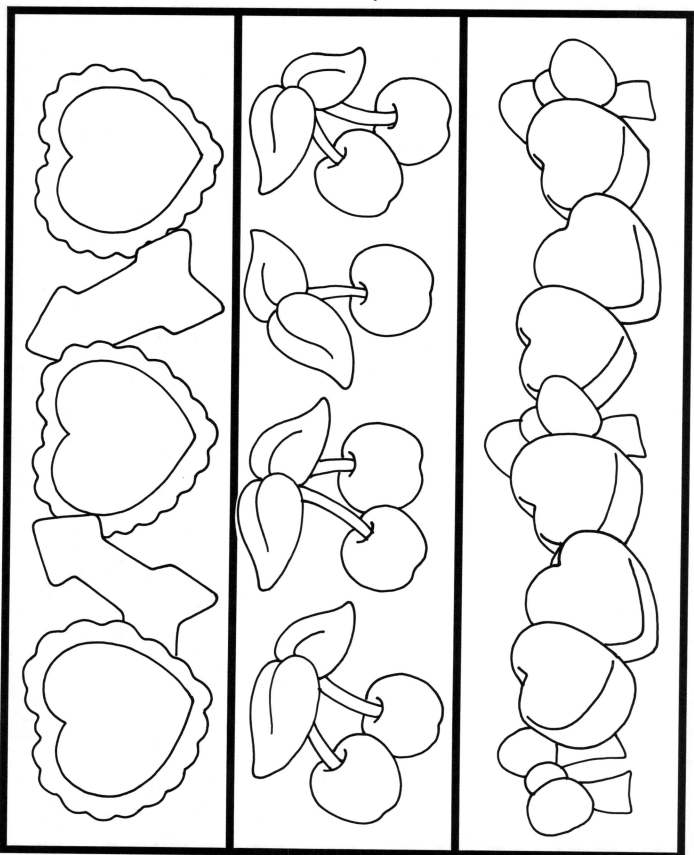

ShortCuts for Winter ©1992 Monday Morning Books, Inc.

Take-Home Progress Notes

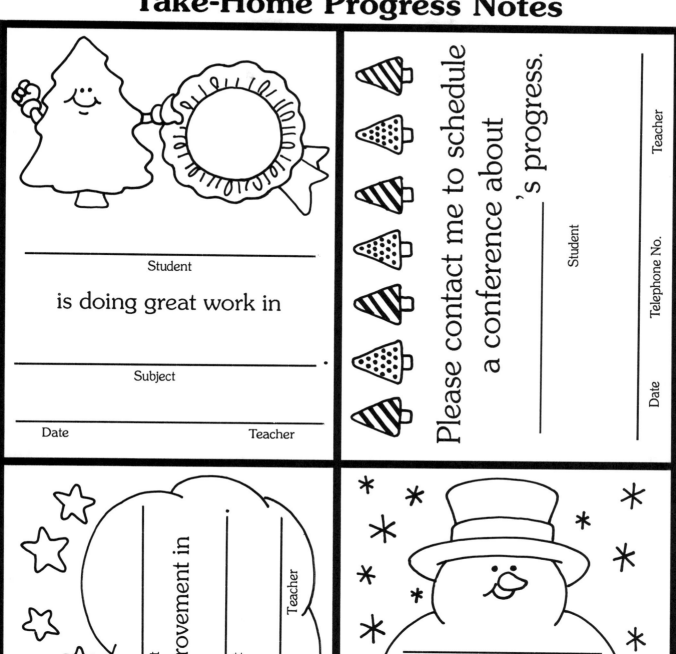

_____
Student

is doing great work in

_____
Subject

Date _____ Teacher _____

Please contact me to schedule a conference about _____'s progress.

_____
Student

Telephone No. _____

Date _____

Teacher _____

_____
Student

has shown improvement in

_____
Subject

Teacher _____

Date _____

_____
Student

needs to improve skills in

_____
Subject

Date _____ Teacher _____

Thank You Notes

Your help is appreciated!

Date

Teacher

VOLUNTEERS ARE GREAT!

Thank you for sharing your time with us!

Teacher

Thank You For All Your Hard Work!

Date

Teacher

Thank you! Thank You!

We couldn't have made it without you!

Teacher

Date

Homework Reminders

Homework Reminder

Due Date

Homework Reminder

Due Date

Homework Reminder

Due Date

Open Notes to Parents

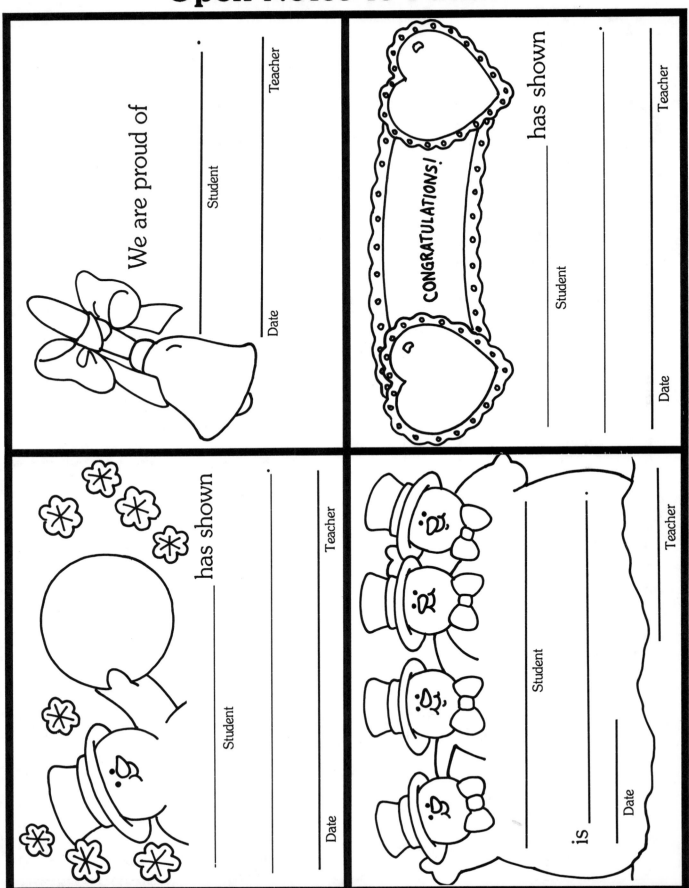

We are proud of

Student

Teacher

Date

CONGRATULATIONS!

has shown

Student

Teacher

Date

has shown

Student

Teacher

Date

has shown

Student

Teacher

Date

is

Open Letter to Parents

Dear Parents,

Planning Calendar

December

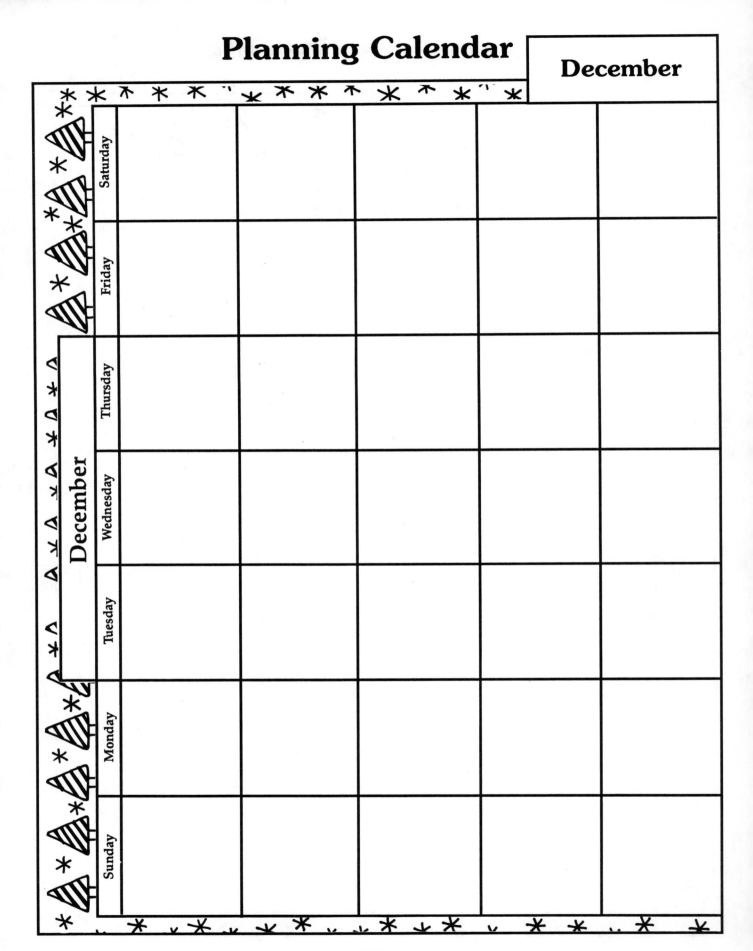

Sunday	Monday	Tuesday	Wednesday	Thursday	Friday	Saturday

Planning Calendar

January

January

Sunday	Monday	Tuesday	Wednesday	Thursday	Friday	Saturday

Planning Calendar

February

	Sunday	Monday	Tuesday	Wednesday	Thursday	Friday	Saturday

Weekly Calendar Frieze
December

MONTH

MONDAY

TUESDAY

WEDNESDAY

THURSDAY

FRIDAY

Weekly Calendar Frieze

January

MONTH

MONDAY

TUESDAY

WEDNESDAY

THURSDAY

FRIDAY

Weekly Calendar Frieze

February

MONTH

MONDAY

TUESDAY

BE MINE

OH YOU CUTIE

WEDNESDAY

THURSDAY

FRIDAY

Birthday Chart
December

DECEMBER
BIRTHDAYS

Birthday Chart
December

HAPPY BIRTHDAY!

Birthday Chart
January

JANUARY BIRTHDAYS

ShortCuts for Winter ©1992 Monday Morning Books, Inc.

Birthday Chart

January

HAPPY BIRTHDAY!

Birthday Chart
February

FEBRUARY BIRTHDAYS

Birthday Chart
February

HAPPY BIRTHDAY!

Scrapbook Page

DECEMBER

Scrapbook Page

JANUARY

Scrapbook Page

FEBRUARY

Seating Chart
December

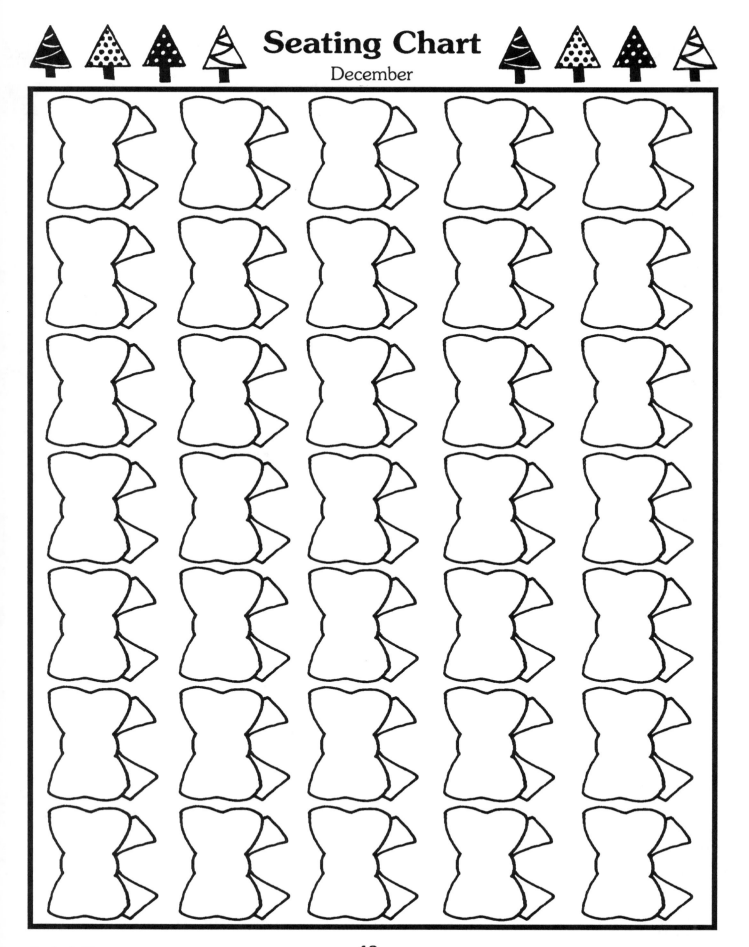

Seating Chart
February

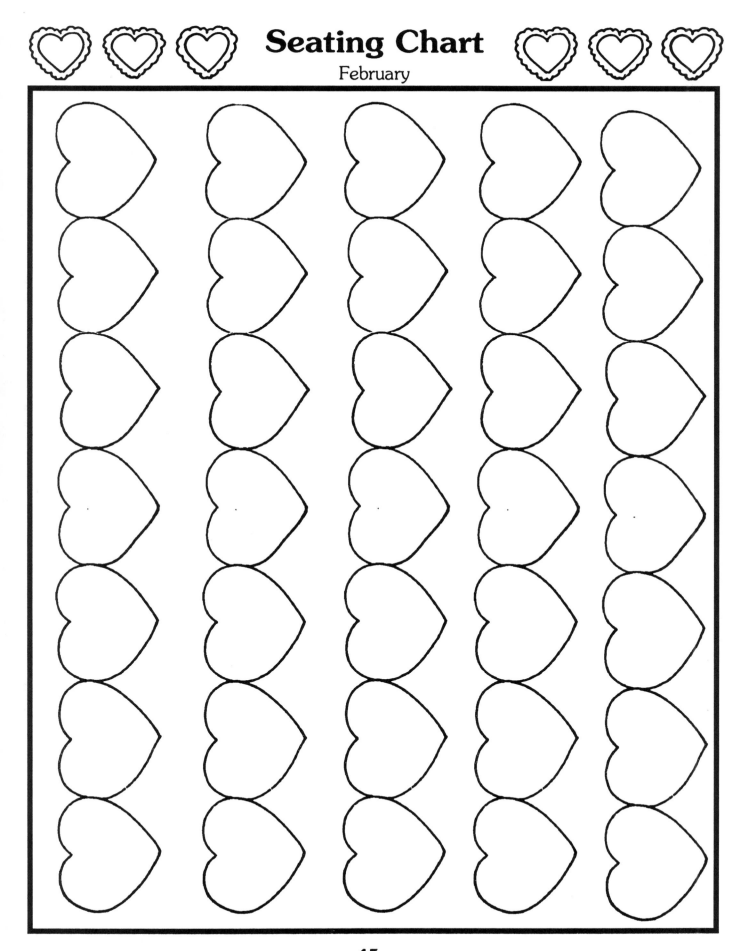

Attendance Chart
December

Name												

Attendance Chart

January

Name												

Attendance Chart

February

Name																		

48

Open Chart

Substitute Teacher Agenda

Lesson Plan   Mr./Ms. _____ Class

_____
_____
_____
_____
_____
_____
_____
_____
_____

Special Information

_____
_____
_____
_____

Students with Special Classes

_____
_____
_____
_____
_____
_____
_____
_____
_____

Classroom Helpers

_____
_____
_____
_____
_____
_____
_____
_____

ShortCuts for Winter ©1992 Monday Morning Books, Inc.

Name _____

Name _____

52

ShortCuts for Winter ©1992 Monday Morning Books, Inc.

Name _____

SUPER!

To display student work,
cut out the banner and
slit along dotted lines.
Then slip worksheet
under paws and secure.

GREAT WORK!

NEW YEAR OF

To display student work, cut out the banner and slit along dotted lines. Then slip worksheet under hands and secure.

Good Work
from
the Heart!

To display student work,
cut out the banner and
slit along dotted lines.
Then slip worksheet
under hands and secure.

Newsletter Cover

Teacher's Name _____ Class

City _____ , State _____

Published _____ times per _____

Newsletter Section Titles

Editorial Staff

In This Issue
NEWS TODAY

A Message From...

EXTRA CREDIT OPPORTUNITIES

The Chatterbox

Welcome Special Guests

Spotlight

Things to Remember

The Letter Box

World News Report

Birthdays

The Kitchen Log

Local News

Homework Hotline

File Folder Cover

December

IN THIS FOLDER

- ☐ Homework
- ☐ Math
- ☐ Social Studies
- ☐ Spelling Words
- ☐ Class Work
- ☐ Science
- ☐ Language Arts
- ☐ Book Report
- ☐ Other _____

File Folder Cover

January

IN THIS FOLDER

☐ Homework

☐ Math

☐ Social Studies

☐ Spelling Words

☐ Class Work

☐ Science

☐ Language Arts

☐ Book Report

☐ Other _____

File Folder Cover
February

IN THIS FOLDER

☐ Homework   ☐ Class Work

☐ Math   ☐ Science

☐ Social Studies   ☐ Language Arts

☐ Spelling Words   ☐ Book Report

☐ Other _____

Name Tags/Flashcards
December

Name Tags/Flashcards

January

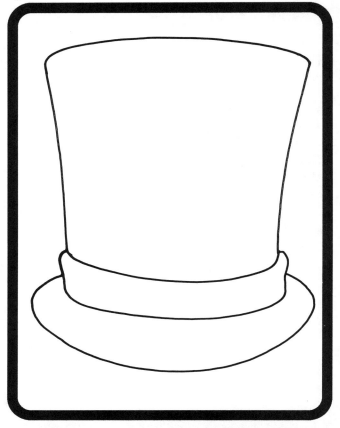
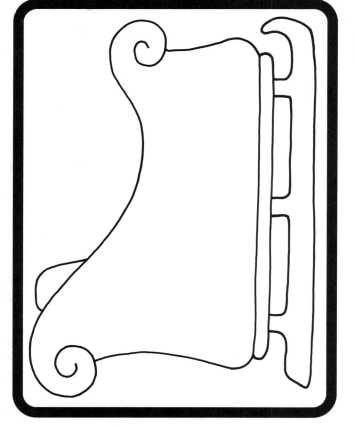

Name Tags/Flashcards
February

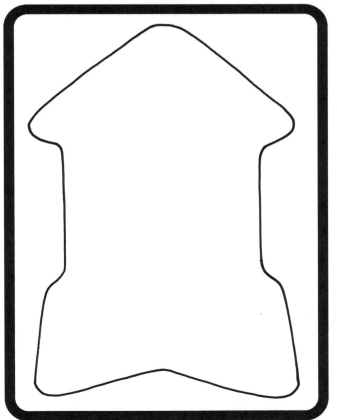

Doorknob Hangers & Hall Passes

ShortCuts for Winter ©1992 Monday Morning Books, Inc.

Bookmarks
Good Books to Read!

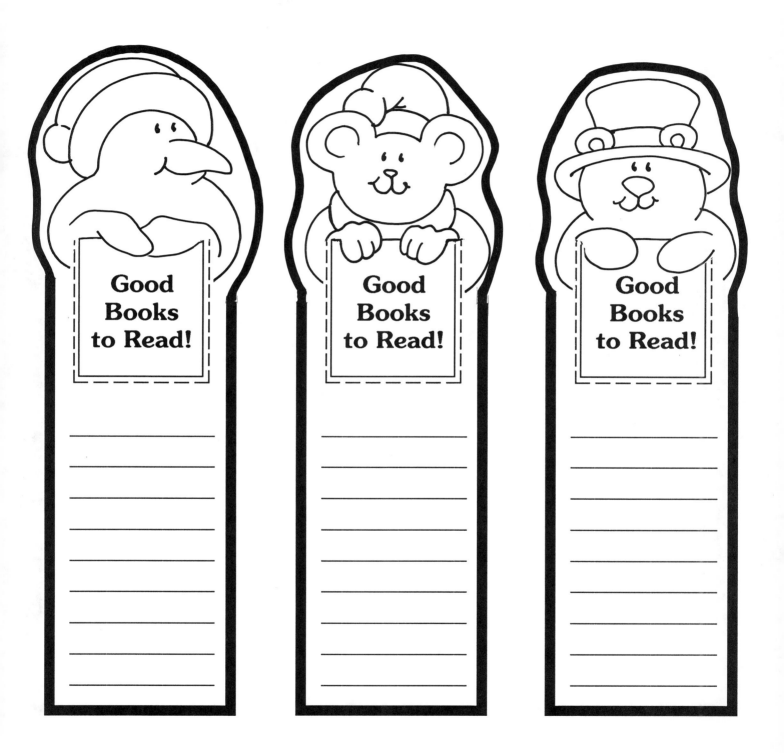

Good
Books
to Read!

Good
Books
to Read!

Good
Books
to Read!

Bookmarks
My Favorite Books

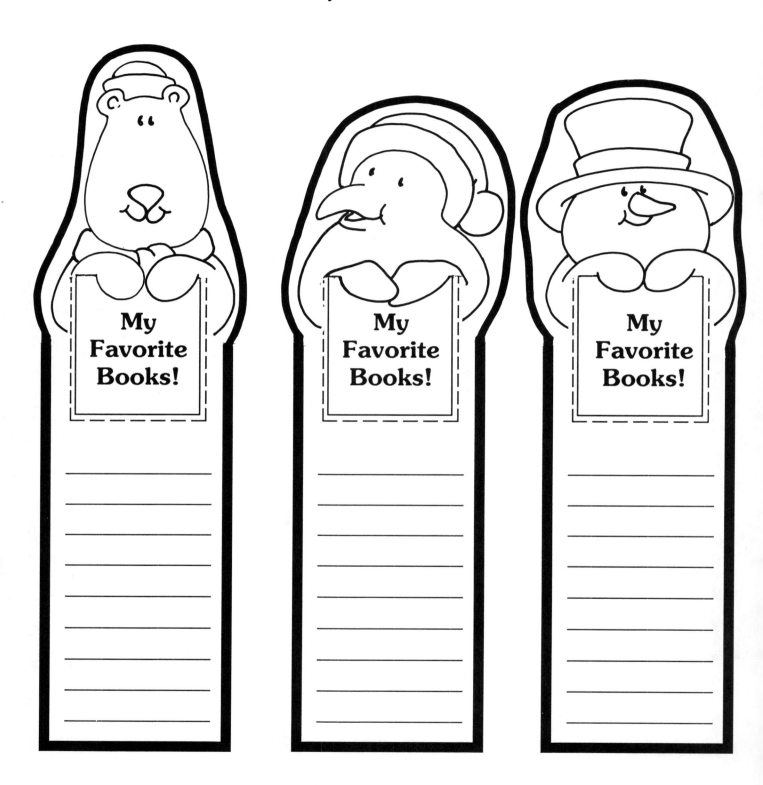

My
Favorite
Books!

My
Favorite
Books!

My
Favorite
Books!

ShortCuts for Winter ©1992 Monday Morning Books, Inc.

Bookmarks
I Love Books!

Pencil Awards
Great Work!

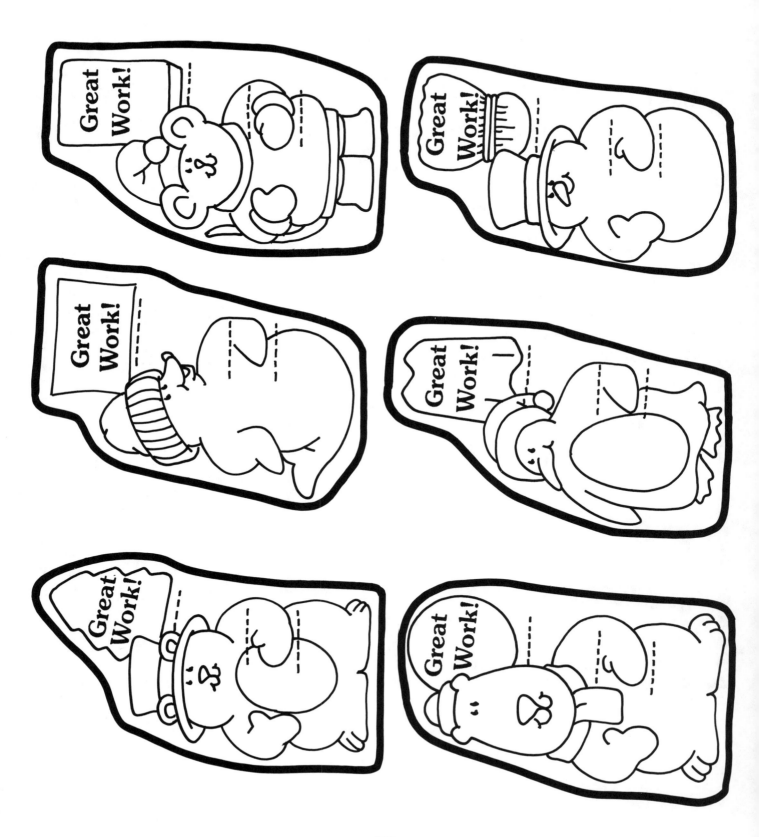

Button Awards
I Do Good Work!

I Do
Good Work!

Name

I Do
Good Work!

Name

I Do
Good Work!

Name

I Do
Good Work!

Name

Button Awards
I Do Good Work!

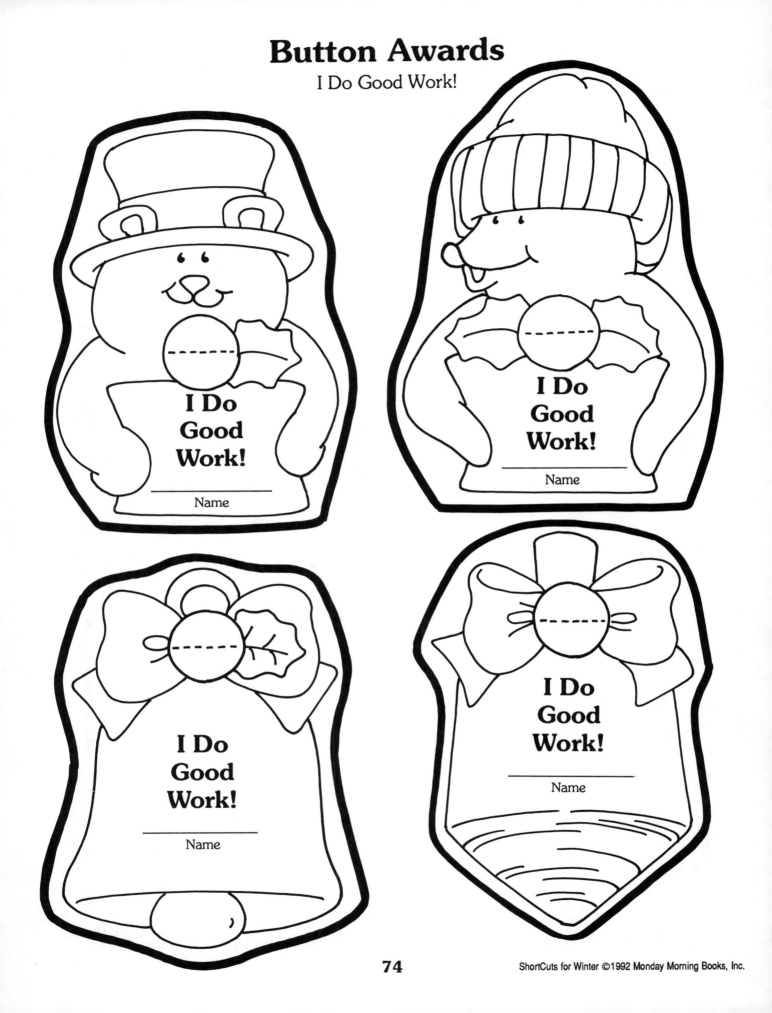

I Do
Good
Work!

Name

I Do
Good
Work!

Name

I Do
Good
Work!

Name

I Do
Good
Work!

Name

Headband/Wristband Awards

Winter

Use Strip **A** for wristband awards.
Use strips **B**, **C**, and **D** for headband awards.

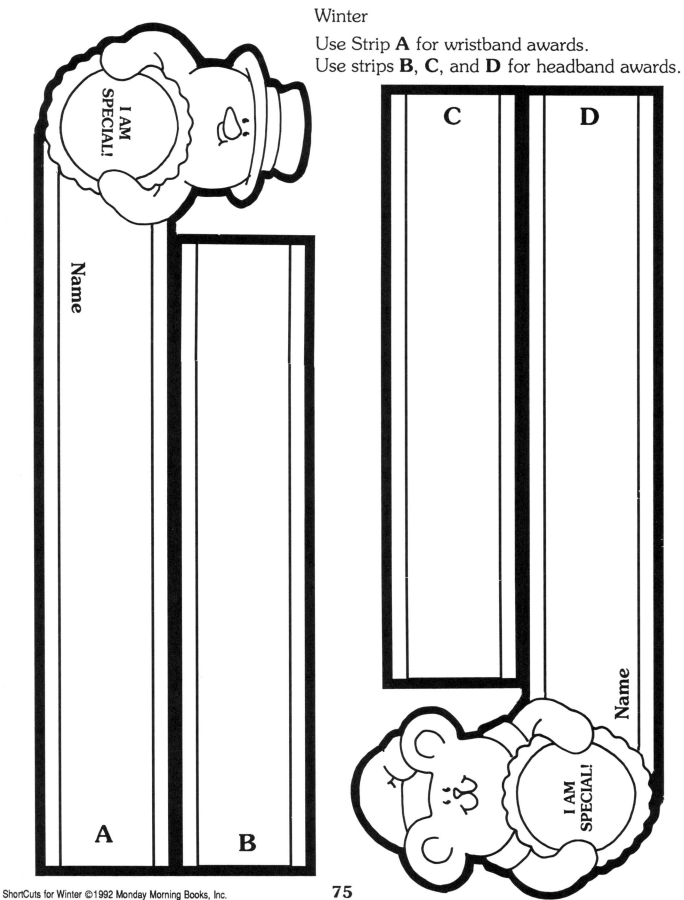

Club Card & Coupon Awards
Winter

North Pole Pals Club Card

_____
Name
is an official member of the
North Pole Pals!

_____
Date   Teacher

North Pole Pals Club Card

_____
Name
is an official member of the
North Pole Pals!

_____
Date   Teacher

North Pole Pals Club Card

_____
Name
is an official member of the
North Pole Pals!

_____
Date   Teacher

North Pole Pals Club Card

_____
Name
is an official member of the
North Pole Pals!

_____
Date   Teacher

North Pole Trading Post
Redeem this coupon for
1 homework
assignment.

North Pole Trading Post
Redeem this coupon for
1 homework
assignment.

North Pole Trading Post
Redeem this coupon for
1 homework
assignment.

North Pole Trading Post
Redeem this coupon for
1 homework
assignment.

Booklet Award
Winter

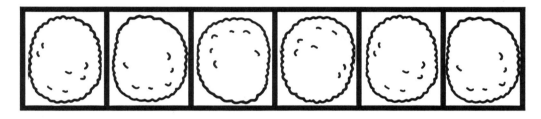

Big Snowflake Diploma

This
BIG SNOWFLAKE
DIPLOMA

is presented to

Name

for

Teacher

Date

SUPER!

Winter Wonderland Diploma

The
Winter Wonderland

DIPLOMA
is presented to

Name

for

Date

Teacher

Big Valentine Diploma

The
Big Valentine

DIPLOMA
is presented to

_____
Name

for _____

_____   _____
Date   Teacher